Welcome to the

menopause

Cover photograph
copyright © Della Reynolds
Illustration by Simon Ellinas
https://www.caricatures.org.uk

My mother didn't talk to me about the menopause, so it all came as a bit of a surprise.

As a working woman in my fifties, I found it difficult to cope with the hot flushes and foggy brain.

Just as no-one tells you much about the arrival of the menopause, no-one can tell you when it will be gone. Is the worse over or is there more to come? Who knows.

So ladies, get your sense of humour sharpened as you are going to need it!

Welcome to the menopause.

Contents

7   Hot Stuff!

9   Cat got sick

11   Make your mind up

14   A lady of a certain age

17   Now that you've gone

21   The bed

24   Neverland

27   Sisters we need proof

30   Letter from a deserted wife

33   Trolley Dolly

37   I am ...

38   The Menopausal Woman's Tinder Ad

40   Over 60's club

42   At first we danced the tango

44   We need to talk

48   Doctor knows best

54   Burn the witch

56   Tell the girl child

59   I am myself (and no-one else)

62   Time

64   The ebb and flow of love

68   Happy Detox

70   Never say never

72   Final word

Hot Stuff!

Hot stuff!

They call me the stripper,
I do it all the time,
On top a double decker,
Or standing in the line.

At a dinner party,
You may think this goes too far,
But before we get the starter,
I'll be sitting in my bra.

Most times out in public,
I'll stop at my strappy vest,
But as the temperature rises,
I can't help but strip the rest.

As others walk in winter,
With mufflers at their throats,
Trying to stay warm,
By buttoning their coats.

I walk out in swimwear,
A bikini or a thong,
If I'm going somewhere formal,
I'll put on a thin sarong.

My thermostat is broken,
Since I stopped the HRT
Now I'm living in the tropics.
Topping 64 degrees.

I can feel the flushes coming,
Starting low down at my feet,
Till my body's radiating,
And I strip off in the heat.

I've tried the old black cohosh,
The red clover and the sage,
It really makes no difference
With my hormones in a rage.

I just can't keep my clothes on,
When I'm sweaty and I'm hot,
So I went to see the doctor,
Stripping clothes off on the spot.

He thought of a solution.
And this is what he did,
He used my heat and power
To boost up the National Grid.

So I plug in every morning,
And the heat it seeps away,
Now I can keep my clothes on.
While I earn some extra pay.

Cat got sick

Cat got sick

Went to vet

Blood test cost

Arm and leg

Dicky thyroid

Too much hormone

Needed pills

Every morning

Cat got hungry

Ate the food

Put on weight

Better mood

Stopped her crying

In the night

Wish I could

Put myself right

First I'm hot

Then I'm cold

Hormone fading

Getting old

She has too much

I've too little

Shame we can't

Meet in the middle.

Make your mind up

Open the window,

Open the door,

Take off jumper,

Throw on the floor.

Put on the fan,

Ramp it up high,

Open the vent,

Let the cool air fly.

Put on jumper,

Wrap it round tight,

Turn off the fan,

Get the fire alight.

Close the window,

Close the door,

Keep in the warmth,

Let the temperature soar.

Put out the fire,

Open the door,

Take off the jumper,

Wipe sweat from each pore,

Open the window,

Turn on the fan,

Put your head in the fridge,

And your feet if you can.

Pull on your socks,

No take them off,

Wrap up in a blanket,

Then strip off.

Turn up the fan,

Then back down low,

Pull on a woolly,

As your goosebumps grow.

First hot then cold,

Without a pause,

I hate this ruddy,

Menopause!

A lady of a certain age

A lady of a certain age,

May just prefer a cuddle,

A hand to hold,

An arm enfold,

Kisses soft and subtle.

What use to her a rampant man,

Who's always keen to squeeze her,

Who wakes at dawn

With full-blown horn,

And promises to please her.

Who hangs around the kitchen,

As she serves up the food

With his ardour

Ever harder,

Hoping that she's in the mood.

So, ladies if you suffer,

From an overactive spouse,

Take my advice

Use his device

To help around the house.

Perhaps you need a bike stand,

A tow bar for a pull

Umbrella hook,

Stand for your book,

Or help with winding wool.

A place to hang your glasses,

While you take your morning shower,

A bagel store,

For three or more

Display a single flower.

Ladies, please do try this,

And if he raves and rants,

Then tell him,

Till you want him,

Just to keep it in his pants.

Now that you've gone

My marriage broke down as I went through the
menopause. I don't think my husband knew any
more than I did about the way the menopause
affects a woman's libido.

Now that you've gone I have;

Soggy lettuce
In a bag,
Two courgettes,
One going bad,
Stale bread ends,
Getting old,
Double sweetcorn,
One with mould,
A pair of leeks,
To make a stew,
When I need-ed one,
Not two.
Double fish cakes,
Double steaks,
Double dinner,
Ready bakes.
Cannot buy,
Dine in for two,
When it's only me,
Not you.
When will Tesco understand,
Not every woman,
Has a man.

Now that you've gone I've lost:

Tea in bed
Not made by me,
Magazines,
Brought home for free.
Someone else,
To light the fire,
Bring in the wood,
Kindle desire.
I must run,
My long, hot bath,
Pour my wine,
Tie my scarf.
Find the shoes,
I want to buy,
Wipe my own tears,
When I cry.
Friend, companion,
Someone to care,
TV pal,
Just being there.

Now that you've gone I've gained:

A double bed,
With room,
To stretch,
No more sleeping,
On the edge.
No more snoring,
No more farts,
And on the sheets,
No more skid marks.
Now it's me,
Who reads in bed.
Controls the light,
Above my head.
No more eating,
Rubbish food,
Just because,
You're in the mood.
No more watching,
Junk TV,
When you don't
Agree with me,
No more rugby,
Cold and grey,
Hoping that,
They'll score,
That day.

But most of all,
Above all this,
No more Guilt,
Is perfect bliss.
No more Sunday morning Guilt,
No more weekend warning Guilt,
No more mini-break away,
Sulking cos I wouldn't play.
No more nagging,
No more dread,
Every time,
I go to bed,
No more need,
To build your ego,
By pandering to,
Your high libido.
Saying no,
Was always wrong,
All in all,
I'm glad you've gone.

The bed

My whole relationship in a single poem.

The bed was ours,
Half yours, half mine.
You had the lamp,
But that was fine.

On winter nights,
You kept me warm,
Snuggled up,
Against the storm.

You'd reach your hand out
In the night,
Just to check,
I was all right.

And when the morning,
Broke the spell,
I'd breath you in,
Absorb your smell.

~~~~~

On clumsy nights,
When you got in,
You'd scratch your toe nail,
Down my shin.

Then intrude
Into my space
With rhythmic snoring,
In my face.

You sprawled across me,
Legs apart.
You'd scratch your arse,
Let out a fart.

Before we knew it,
Each night we found,
The bed became
A battle ground.

~~~~~

And now you've gone,
The bed is mine,
I have the lamp,
And that is fine.

It took me months,
Before I tried,
To roll across,
On to your side.

Then many more,
Till I was able.
To put my drink,
On your side table,

Or save the walk
Around the bed,
Get in and out,
your side instead.

I needed time,
To re-adjust
To being me,
No longer us.

Neverland

You were Peter Pan,
I was your Wendy.
We would fly to Neverland
Forever young and trendy.

You put a ring on my finger
And off we flew together
To keep our promise
And stay the same forever.

But pretty soon the fairy dust,
Of love was not enough,
My body starting changing,
You found it pretty tough.

My bouts of cystitis,
Interrupted the passion,
You were unhappy that,
Your pleasures were on ration.

Then my hot flushes
made it difficult to fly,
I couldn't keep up with you,
No matter how I tried.

My elasticated trousers,
Upset your equilibrium,
You told me not to,
Ever leave the house in them.

And when I wanted PJs,
For comfort in the night,
You put your foot down,
And said it wasn't right.

All this comfort dressing,
Was just me letting go,
Where were my skinny jeans
You wanted to know.

Invasive arthritis
Buggered up my knee,
Made me walk with stiffness,
Like I was ninety three.

As I coped with those hot flushes,
Arthritis in my bones,
A fading libido,
A love of staying home.

You took off to the stars,
And left me far behind,
And found a brand new Wendy,
The eternal youthful kind.

During our time together,
Ten years or more had gone,
I'm sorry I got older,
And spoiled all the fun.

Sisters we need proof!

The more I thought about it the more unfair I found it. My body had naturally changed as I moved through my 50's yet I got the feeling that I should somehow be able to 'mend' myself and turn back the clock.

Where is it written
That a woman must stay smitten,
To the man she wed?

Where is it recorded,
That a woman is applauded,
If she delivers in bed?

Where is the data,
That she's a man-hater,
If she says no instead?

Did they do a survey
Is it in our DNA,
Was it written in the bible,
What do the experts say?

Can you find it in a blood test,
Or see it in a scan,
Is there any evidence,
Women make love like a man?

Where is the science
That she's designed to be compliant,
To her man's desire?

Where is the credo,
Which states that her libido,
Is continually on fire?

Where is the legislation,
That she'll have no hesitation,
To remove her attire?

All I know is my own chemistry,
Stripped of its hormones,
And denied HRT

Listen to your body,
My counsellor will say,
And my body tells me,
It no longer wants to play.

My juices have run dry,
There's no electricity,
But the world gangs up,
To say there's something wrong with me.

I should summon up my passion,
Do my duty as a wife,
I will be dysfunctional
Without a vigorous sex life.

So sisters do you feel it,
Do you feel the same as me?
Then we need to see the evidence,
And set each other free.

I think that it's an urban myth,
A perpetuated sham,
That a menopausal woman should have
The sex drive of a man.

Letter from a deserted wife

Dear Absent Husband,

It was handy that you left me,
Just before I stopped HRT
Cos the night sweats really hit me,
And I couldn't sleep in bed.

So I had to move to your side,
Then I had to roll on mine,
To try and find a cool spot,
I was turning all the time.

One minute covers on me,
Then, all pushed on the mat,
My arms and legs akimbo,

No, you wouldn't have liked that.

It was lucky you departed,
Before arthritis started,
Just where my knee bone parted,
And caused me so much pain.

My back went into spasm,
That's quite common I am told,
And I shuffled round the house,
Like a woman bent and old.

So I had to move the TV,
To lay down my yoga mat,
So I could ease the stiffness,

No, you wouldn't have liked that.

A most fortuitous plan,
To walk out before the scan,
And the treatment all began,
For the cancer in my breast.

For after operation,
No fondling was allowed,
I had to sleep in clothing,
And I know we would have rowed.

Because the hormone blockers
Make you moody, make you fat,
And I wouldn't feel seductive,

No, you wouldn't have liked that.

So much for the vow
Of sickness and in health,
I guess that when you made it,
You were thinking of yourself.

When I reached my sell by date,
It seems you didn't hesitate,
To trade in for a brand new mate,

Now, who wouldn't have liked that?

Trolley Dolly

My husband had an aversion to my wicker basket
shopping trolley.

He said it wasn't sexy,
He said it wasn't cool,
To go shopping with my trolley,
(My wicker basket trolley),
A girl out on the pull.

When I took it out to Tesco,
He would walk ten feet behind,
And he'd never touch the trolley,
(My wicker basket trolley),
So I had to change his mind.

One evening at the theatre,
I knew just the thing to do,
Saw potential in my trolley,
(My wicker basket trolley),
To create a sexual stew.

The next time we went shopping,
I would give him a surprise,
And show him that my trolley,
(My wicker basket trolley),
Could transform before his eyes.

It was in the central isle,
Between the cornflakes and the Daz,
That I revealed my trolley,
(My wicker basket trolley),
Could deliver all that Jazz.

As the music hit the airwaves,
I exposed my fishnet thigh,
Took stilettos from my trolley
(My wicker basket trolley),
And I looked him in the eye.

Then I threw my trolley backwards
Dragging it across the floor,
Lifting legs astride my trolley,
(My wicker basket trolley),
As I straddled it some more.

Come on babe why don't we paint the town,
I whispered sexily,
As my heel flipped up my trolley,
(My wicker basket trolley),
And I caught it on my knee.

Then everyone joined in,
With a shimmy and a shake,
As I draped across my trolley,
(My wicker basket trolley),
Gliding past the ready bake.

Then holding on the handle,
Tipped my head back to the floor,
Kicked each leg out from my trolley.
(My wicker basket trolley),
As the crowd called out for more.

I performed a single back flip,
Wicker basket in the air,
Landing square onto my trolley,
(My wicker basket trolley),
Running fingers through my hair.

By now he was just staring,
He could not believe his eyes,
They were fixed upon my trolley,
(My wicker basket trolley),
Caught between my fishnet thighs.

Now upon the weekend,
He'll put on his black string vest,
And he'll run to fetch the trolley,
(My wicker basket trolley),
And I'm sure you know the rest.

I am:

A barren woman,
A spinster,
Abandoned wife,
A failed vegetarian,
11+ reject,
Invisible,
Menopausal
Woman.
Men have called me,
Selfish,
Unfeeling,
Detached,
Frigid,
But that's just on my bad days.

I'm also ...
Inventive
Creative,
Problem solver,
Resourceful,
Thoughtful,
Independent,
Analytical,
Political,
Critical,
Risk taker,
Cat lover,
Poem writer,
Strong fighter
Survivor.
Perception is a wonderful thing.

37

The Menopausal Woman's
Tinder Ad

I do Tai Chi,
Don't mess with me,
And I'm not taking
HRT

I know my own mind,
I am strong,
I've compromised,
For far too long.

I don't do bullshit,
Conversation,
Flirting comments,
Adoration.

Won't massage feet,
Or stroke male ego,
Won't change my clothes,
Because you say so.

I'm no longer
Sexually active,
I've had enough,
Of looking attractive.

Of pampering,
My hair and nails,
Skinny jeans,
And killer heels.

Of worrying,
Will my partner blank me,
If I say no,
To hanky panky.

I don't need clitoral,
Stimulation,
Prefer you tickle,
My imagination.

With all that said,
You never know,
If you're up for a challenge,
Then give it a go.

The over 60's club

Mature dating can be fraught with
misunderstandings!

I was looking for friendship,
Not for love,
When I joined
The over 60's club.

I met an architect called Mike,
But I soon told him 'on your bike'.
He clearly had designs on me,
At the over 60's club.

The decorator guy came next,
But he was just a sexual pest,
I told him not to size me up,
At the over 60's club.

Then on a walk, I tell you straight
I met old Pete a plumber's mate,
He took my hand while we were sitting,
To show me his compression fitting.
At the over 60's club.

At bingo in-between the calls,
As Dave the postman spun the balls,
I didn't know just what to say,
When his oversize package came my way.
At the over 60's club.

I met a sparky called Old Stan,
Who said that he was just the man,
Resistance was futile, he knew,
To a man skilled in the Edison Screw.
At the over 60's club.

Then at a tea dance last weekend,
I had a waltz with my new friend,
Bert the mechanic caused some ripples,
When he said he'd like to grease my nipples.
At the over 60's club.

A manager from Eurostar,
Said, stick with him and I'd go far,
All the way, top notch, first class,
If I show him my special …
pass
At the over 60's club.

At the disco I gyrate with Greg,
A carpenter with nimble legs,
He said he had a special move,
And closed in for a tongue and groove.
At the over 60's club.

Then finally, the other day,
I met our Vince and he was gay,
So now we dance and walk and play.
At the over 60's club.

At first we danced the tango

Relationships work when you are both dancing to
the same tune.

At first we danced the tango,
When the passion roused your ardour,
With the promise of forever,
You held me ever harder.

When we entered into foxtrot,
You adjusted to my pace,
Happy to be guided
By my welcoming embrace.

At the waltz you started quipping,
That the action was too slow,
Why not do a paso doble?
Why not let our bodies go?

But when the music started
For the menopause bolero
You tired of the dancing
And your interest fell to zero.

You wanted to return
To the passion of before,
Swing your partner to a samba,
Do a quickstep round the floor.

With fast collapsing arches
And a body hot, then cold
I could not dance to your tune,
Though you pleaded and cajoled.

And I thought my dancing days,
Were over when you left
But now I've come to realise that,
There's rhythm in me yet.

So I need a new dance partner,
Someone who understands,
That a menopausal woman,
Needs a gentle, guiding hand.

We need to talk

Things we just don't talk about in social company

Politics

Religion

Our annual salary.

So, we never close the pay gap,

Which is hidden out of view,

Never challenge our convictions,

Whether red or blue,

And we never ask the question

Of how a loving God,

Created life to eat each other,

Which is really rather odd.

And while we're on the subject,

There are other things taboo,

That we can't share with others,

To get their point of view.

I would like to raise the subject,

Between courses over supper.

Of how to spice my sex life,

So it doesn't come a cropper.

How do all my friends cope,

When they've been a long time wed,

Trying to ring the changes,

In the same old marital bed.

Do they dress up as nurses,

Or in silky lingerie,

Or try a bit of bondage,

As in 50 shades of grey.

Do they use chocolate sauce,

Or cans of squirty cream,

Nipple clamps or bollock cramps,

To make their partner scream.

We chat across the cheeseboard,

As we all enjoy the brie,

But it's just about safe topics

Like yesterday's TV.

So, if I can't ask the question,

I can only guess,

That just like me they always try,

To do their very best.

To convince the thrill of romance,

Is the reason they're together,

When more likely it's the mortgage,

And a fear of finding better.

And all the time it's secret,

And we never know what's true,

We think that we're the only one,

Who hasn't got a clue.

Doctor knows best

After an operation for breast cancer the follow
up treatment was set to mess up my hormones
even more than the menopause had done.

So, here's the deal,

You're 61,

Getting on,

But more to come.

We found a tumour,

Took it out,

Good clean edges,

Round about.

So now we go into phase two,

And this is what,

We do for you.

We take high energy radiation,

And zap your cells,

Into mutation.

This will destroy

The DNA,

Of any cells,

Caught in the way.

This causes damage,

To your lung,

Will weaken bones,

Shall I go on?

Will make you tired,

Will make you sore,

Could cause hair loss,

And there is more.

The radiation

We pump through,

Might clip your heart,

It does a few,

Your arm may swell,

Your shoulder stiffen,

Will make you weak,

Now that's a given.

And once we've done,

With zapping tissue,

We give you pills,

On regular issue.

They block your hormones,

Make you fat,

For just five years,

You can live with that.

Your joints will hurt,

Your muscles achy,

Your hair and nails,

Will go all flaky.

Your bones will thin,

You may get fractures,

Hypertension,

Itchy patches.

Fatigue, low mood and dizzy spells,

Your brain will fog,

Your wrists may swell.

The menopause,

Will dry you up,

But you can use,

That jelly stuff.

Night sweats, hot flushes,

First hot, then colder

You will soon feel,

Ten years older.

It's not all bad,

Don't be downhearted,

Just sign the form.

And we'll get started.

What's that you say,

Why hesitate,

We're helping your

Survival rate.

We'll give you other medication,

For side effects

From what you're taking.

Just sign here on

The dotted line,

Trust in us,

That all is fine.

So you reject the help we're giving,

Say sod survival,

That's not living.

We understand,

That you're ignoring,

Our advice

But heed our warning.

No radiation,

No backup pills,

You run the risk,

That you'll get ill!

Burn the witch

Menopausal women can be very knowing.

Burn the witch,
Burn the witch,
The bolshy old woman,
She knows too much.

She knows how to cure the sick,
Just by mixing herbs and sticks.
Must surely be the devil's work,
When we wise men can't heal the hurt.

Burn the witch,
Burn the witch,
She lived too long,
And can't be tricked.

She knows that we the patriarchs,
Don't know our elbow from our arse.
That we rule by bluff and swagger,
She sees right through our empty blather.

Burn the witch,
Burn the witch,
For having thoughts,
Beyond our reach.

Just by being she bends our truth,
Offends our eyes, with loss of youth.
What use a woman without a man,
To give her purpose on this land.

Burn the witch,
Burn the witch,
Or hand her high,
And watch her twitch.

And let the burning be a warning.
To any woman not conforming.

Tell the girl child

Our programming begins young.

Tell the girl child

She's just not enough.

She must be more beautiful

If she wants to be loved.

Tell her that her eyes,

Which can pierce a man's soul,

Are dull and lifeless,

Without mascara and kohl.

Tell her that her lips,

Luscious and smooth,

Able to excite,

Able to soothe,

Tell her that those lips,

So perfect a pout,

Must be covered in lipstick,

Before she goes out.

Tell her that her skin,

Sensuous to touch,

Must hide behind makeup

Powder and puff.

Tell her that her breasts,

Orbs of perfection,

Are too small, or too large,

To be of satisfaction.

Tell her that her curves,

Which sashay with rhythm,

And light sparks of fire,

Should really be hidden.

Whatever you do,

Don't tell her the truth.

That men lose their power,

To feminine youth.

That natural beauty,

Destroys their control,

Obsessed by desire,

They would give you

Their soul.

No tell her the lie,

And tell it her young.

It will last all her life,

Now the damage is done.

I am myself
(and no-one else)

I wish I knew you sooner.

Being a thumb-sucking, knocked-kneed kid,

Disguised your potential.

You stood on the side-line of life,

I should have invited you in.

I recall your twenties,

You found your first love,

Thinking it your last love,

For love lasts forever right?

I was there at your wedding,

And there at your divorce.

When you lay in the bath,

As the water went cold,

And the tears ran dry,

I lay there with you.

I felt every heave of your heart,

Every twist of your gut,

I held you in the darkness,

When no-one else was there.

In your mid-life, you lived dangerously.

Exploring your sensuality.

Finding for the first time,

How utterly appealing you could be.

I am the only person,

Who has never left you,

After promising to stay.

Now in the hinterland of life,

I know you so well,

And trust your strength so intensely,

That darkness can hold no fear.

I wish I knew that sooner.

Time

Butter turns rancid,

Bread become mouldy

Flowers drop petals,

Socks become holey.

The passage of time,

Like divine intervention,

Reduces my love life,

To habitual convention.

The hands which caressed me,

Now deploy a flip action,

To change my position,

For his satisfaction.

The kisses are brief,

The cuddles are token,

The sweet words of love,

Are no longer spoken.

No-one's to blame.

Passions will fade.

It's beyond our control,

Just as night turns to day.

So, bake some fresh bread,

And buy some more butter,

When romance goes stale,

Time to take a new lover.

The ebb and flow of love:

When I was 6 there was no kiss.

No comfort hug,

No look of love,

No soft caress,

Just loneliness,

Was all I knew.

When I was 16 I got the look.

The look of lust.

It made me warm,

It made me feel,

It made me real,

For the first time.

When I was 26 it seemed like love.

As I disrobed,

As I partook,

Of touch and smell,

Of body warmth.

I took my comfort there.

When I was 36 I took for granted,

The look of love,

The touch of love,

The warmth of love,

The being of love.

I was accepted.

When I was 46 it all slowed down.

But still I held,

The love of man,

The touch of man,

The warmth of man.

I felt loved.

When I was 56 the lust left me.

And with it went,

The love of man,

The soft caress,

The touch of hands,

I was rejected.

At 66 there is no kiss,

No comfort hug,

No look of love,

No soft caress,

Just loneliness.

Was it ever love?

Happy Detox

If you are thinking of shifting some of that
menopausal muffin top, here is some advice for
you.

Going on a detox diet?
Things to do before you try it.

Temptation must be kept at bay,
Take all forbidden foods away.

Eat the chocolate, eat the sweets,
Eat the crips and eat the treats.

Now your cupboards are detox clean,
Soon you'll be a lean machine.

Next stop, polish off the booze,
Opened bottle must be used.

Drink the wine and drink the gin,
Nearly ready to begin.

Dairy's not a good idea,
So finish up the butter dear.

Spread it thick onto your toast,
Ooze on crumpets, smear on roasts.

The cheese you can consume on crackers,
Once you detox, no more snackers.

And knowing meat just can't be taken,
Make triple-deckers with the bacon.

Now watch those extra pounds fall off,
Once there are no snacks to scoff.

It may not always work first time.
Don't be disheartened, all is fine.

If you increase instead of slimming,
Just start again from the beginning.

Happy Detox!

Never say never

Discarded like an old dry leaf,

I lay,

Knowing my limitations.

Time had stolen my youth,

Age tweaked at my bones.

More desirable women had tempted away

My lover.

Then we met.

A casual encounter.

I put up no resistance for that would indicate

An expectation beyond my worth.

I lived in the moment,

As one moment followed another.

Through your eyes I saw myself anew,

Through your touch I felt myself awaken.

Your fingertips sculptured my body into

Desirable shapes.

Curves and undulations became wildly seductive.

As your appreciative hand traced

long- forgotten contours.

I saw the reflection of my beauty

In your beholder's eye.

It is not too late.

No ladies, it is not too late.

There is life beyond the menopause and men who understand the need to be a bit more inventive in the bedroom.

It's not all bad. The menopause brings with it liberation from emotional/sexual turmoil. You are at peace with who you are and receive a boost to your brain power and creativity.

The subject of the menopause is becoming less taboo and by sharing our experiences we can support the sisterhood. So make sure you buy a copy of this book for all your menopausal friends and get the conversation going.

I will leave you with my favourite line and the one which neatly sums up the way to a menopausal woman's heart.

Printed in Great Britain
by Amazon